WANT TO KNOW THE TRUTH ABOUT THE VILE VICTORIANS?

read on!

Read this bit first...!

Here at Truth or Busted Headquarters, when WE think of the Victorians the following things come to mind:

Top hats (or super tall, stovepipe hats), monocles, waxed moustaches like bicycle handlebars, long black dresses and bonnets...

Smoke-filled factories, crumbling slums, gloomy workhouses and lots of poo...

Stuffy, pompous, stern-faced, chamber-pot-using, straight-laced folk who didn't enjoy life — or wouldn't admit it if they did!

And YOU, are you sitting up straight while you read this book? (The Victorians thought slouching was a sign of an undisciplined mind!)

There are lots of opinions about the Victorians that conform to this view. For example:

- ☆ *Queen Victoria was not amused.*
- ☆ *Victorian children should be seen and not heard.*
- ☆ *Victorian people went to church religiously every Sunday.*
- ☆ *Small boys were sent to work up chimneys.*

But are they Truth or Busted? Read on and you'll find out the answers to these and a whole lot more!

In *Truth or Busted: Victorian Workers Turned Dog Poo Into Gold* we will also explore the (at times) wild, weird and wacky world of the Victorians. By the time you've finished you'll be an expert with enough facts rattling inside your head to send your friends into a deep sleep or thrill them into writing a super-brainiac essay on the Victorians!

So, if you want to know the truth about stuff like:

- ☆ *Did Victorians wash their clothes in wee...?*
- ☆ *Did Victorian girls glow in the dark...?*
- ☆ *Did Victorian boys really wear dresses...?*

... then *Truth or Busted: Victorian Workers Turned Dog Poo Into Gold* is for you!

read on!

Queen Victoria was not amused

Poor old Queen Victoria (1819–1901) is supposed to have said 'We are not amused' when a courtier told her a spicy story at dinner. This wasn't reported until 20 years after her death, but the 'dour and humourless' label stuck like glue to the Queen.

To make matters worse, most of the photos we see of Victoria seem to confirm this gloomy view. They show her looking grim-faced and usually dressed from head to toe in black.

So what's going on? Was Queen Vic really an old misery guts?

★ And the truth is...

Look at most Victorian photographs... almost everyone looks miserable! In those days people wanted formal, dignified images. Grinning madly for the camera came along in the 20th century.

Added to this, for much of her life Victoria actually was quite sad. She was devoted to her husband, Prince Albert, and was heartbroken when he died in 1861. After his death she wore black clothes, to show she was in mourning, for the rest of her life.

BUT that's only part of the story. Victoria reigned for so long that people have forgotten she was lively and vivacious as a young Queen. When she first met Albert she wrote in her diary:

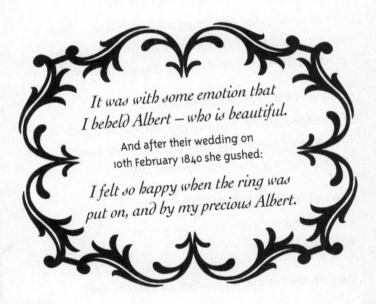

It was with some emotion that I beheld Albert — who is beautiful.

And after their wedding on 10th February 1840 she gushed:

I felt so happy when the ring was put on, and by my precious Albert.

Verdict: **BUSTED**

VICTORIA IN LOVE

Queen Victoria kept a diary from the tender age of 13 until her death. It filled 43,000 pages. In her diary, Victoria's love for Albert shines through:

1840 ALBERT AND THEIR WEDDING

He clasped me in his arms, and we kissed each other again and again! His beauty, his sweetness and gentleness — how can I ever be thankful enough...

1861 AFTER ALBERT'S DEATH

Have been unable to write my journal since the day my beloved one left us, and with a heavy broken heart I enter a new year without him...

1863 STILL HEARTBROKEN

Here I sit lonely and desolate, who so needs love and tenderness...

Dare we tell her she has another 40 years to live?

FLABBERGASTATION!

DODGY VICTORIAN DINNERS

I say!

Most Victorians really did work hard, and often had tough manual jobs like miners, ironworkers, mill girls or domestic servants. This meant they had to eat a lot of food for energy — in fact many Victorian labourers ate around twice as much as people do today.

To save money, some of their food was awful — ooops — offal. Offal is the 'delicious' and tastebud-tantalising internal organs of animals. The brains, heart, intestines, lungs, liver, kidneys, sweetbreads and tongue were particular favourites of the Victorian people.

Hang on, sweetbreads? They sound delicious — are they a croissant, or perhaps a sweet pastry? No such luck. Sweetbreads are the pancreas or thyroid gland of calves or lambs. Victorians would grill or fry them with bacon for a yummy teatime treat.

How about a lovely plate of tripe? That'll be the stomach lining of a cow — boiled, bleached, frilly and white — all seasoned with lashings of salt and pepper.

And don't forget the fish: herrings — soused, dried, pickled or smoked — sprats, eels and oysters, mussels, cockles and whelks. Not a fish scale was wasted — heads, tails, skins and little crunchy bones were all munched down. Yum!

9

Gladstone was a mad Prime Minister

Queen Victoria's favourite Prime Minister was Benjamin Disraeli. When 'Dizzy' lost the 1868 election to William Gladstone, the Queen was outraged. She thought Gladstone was quite mad! But was this justified?

★ And the truth is...

Gladstone was a great Liberal Prime Minister. He was elected four times between 1868 and 1894. However, for a politician, he had some strange hobbies:

☆ In 1858, he took up tree felling and kept his axe sharpened until the ripe old age of 81.

☆ At night he walked the streets of London without a bodyguard. His mission was to talk to prostitutes who lived on the streets and persuade them to lead better lives.

☆ He spent hours each day reading and consumed over 21,000 books during his lifetime.

Verdict: **BUSTED**

The Victorian dead travelled by train

During the Victorian era, a high-speed 'dead train' ferried corpses from the northern English port of Hull to Cambridge, in the south. These pale passengers* weren't going on holiday or commuting to work — so where was their final destination?

 ## And the truth is...

Cambridge University ran a medical school, and every student was required to dissect two bodies. The university couldn't get enough local corpses, so they transported them in from Hull.

Body dealers bought the dead and stored them in leak-proof coffins. This eerie cargo was loaded onto late-night 'dead' trains and transported to the university! English medical schools bought around 125,000 bodies between 1832 and 1930.

Verdict: **TRUTH**

* this is a *Truth or Busted* euphemism for 'dead passengers'

> ## Queen Victoria was so popular they named the era after her

In her later years Queen Victoria was deeply respected and loved by her people. During her Diamond Jubilee in 1897 the entire British Empire celebrated. As a mark of respect, 46,000 troops paraded through London, including Bengal Lancers from India and fierce Dayak head hunters from Borneo. In Manchester, a breakfast party was held for 100,000 lucky children to celebrate their Queen.

So, it's true then... Victoria was really very popular?

And the truth is...

Not the whole way through her reign!

When the young Princess Victoria first became to the throne, the monarchy was not popular at ALL. Not one bit. Her uncle George IV had wasted a fortune, while his brother William IV was known as 'Silly Billy'. In fact, the general feeling towards the monarchy was not very positive.

Amazingly, between the decades of 1840 and 1882, there were eight attempts on the life of Queen Victoria. She was shot at seven times, but luckily only one would-be killer had a properly loaded gun — and he missed. The only time the Queen was actually hurt was in 1850, when she was hit over the head with a heavy cane by a deranged ex-cavalry officer called Robert Pate, who went mad when his favourite horse was put down. The attack crushed Victoria's bonnet and drew blood.

After the death of her beloved Prince Albert in 1861, the Queen rarely appeared in public and people began to ask if there was any point to the monarchy. By 1870 there were more than 50 clubs across Britain calling for a republic (this is a system of government without a king or queen). However, from the 1870s onwards, people began to change their minds. As she grew older Queen Victoria came to be seen as the grandmother of the Empire. Her people warmed to her and she became more and more popular.

Verdict: __BUSTED__ (mostly)

Corporal Punishment

During the Victorian era, physical punishment was given out for the mildest of misdemeanours...

Teachers caned their pupils – some even kept their favourite stick in a bucket of water so it was always supple and ready for whipping action! Other teachers preferred the 'tawse', which was a leather strap that was split into a number of tails at the end and could deliver painful red welts to the legs or arms. In 1860 a particularly vicious Victorian teacher was convicted of manslaughter and sentenced to just four years in jail for beating a 14-year-old boy to death!

Violent criminals or vagrants (another name for homeless people) could be punished with a flogging as well as (or instead of) going to prison. Younger offenders were hit with a stick called the birch, and records show that 4,116 young people were 'birched' in 1900 alone.

Women had to watch themselves, too. Many Victorian men believed they had the right to beat their wives – as long they used a stick. If violent husbands came before the courts they usually got away with a fine.

> # Queen Victoria blamed her son for her husband's death

Queen Victoria was not a fan of her eldest son, Edward (known as Bertie). In 1862 she wrote in a letter to her eldest daughter:

'That boy. I can never look at him without a shudder.'

It seems she despised Bertie — but why?

 And the truth is...

Bertie was a bit of a tearaway. While he was at Cambridge University, some friends fixed him up with a girlfriend, an actress by the name of Nelly Clifden. Albert found out and was furious. He feared blackmail or a major royal scandal.

Albert was already ill with severe stomach pains, fever and diarrhoea, but he hurried to see Bertie in Cambridge to make his feelings known. After a long walk together through the city in the pouring rain, they reached an understanding.

However, when Albert returned to Windsor he became even sicker, and three weeks later he died.

Rightly or wrongly Victoria never forgave Bertie.

Verdict:  TRUTH

The Victorians invented the black cab

Have you ever stood on a street and waved for a taxi? Yep. Then you've used a *hackney* or *black cab*. Everyone assumes they were a Victorian invention — but is that the case?

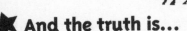

⭐ And the truth is...

The first hackney carriages operated in the early 17th century. Captain John Baily put four coaches to work by the Maypole Inn in the Strand in 1634, which was London's first cab rank.

By the 19th century most hackney cabs were four-wheeled carriages, pulled by two horses and carrying up to six people.

The great Victorian innovation was the Hansom cab. Hansoms were two-wheeled and pulled by a single horse. They were light, fast and agile. The cab sat two passengers inside, with the driver on a high, sprung seat behind them. He was paid through a flap in the roof and had a mechanism to keep the door locked till he had the cash.

So it was the *Hansom* cab that was a symbol of the Victorian age, not the *hackney* cab.

Verdict: **BUSTED**

VILE VICTORIANS!

The Duke of Wellington

Prime Minister: 1828–1830

Claim to fame: Beat Napoleon at the Battle of Waterloo in 1815.

Nickname: *The Iron Duke.*

Reason: He put iron shutters over the windows of his London home to stop rioters breaking the glass.

Sir Robert Peel

Prime Minister: 1841–1846

Claim to fame: Founded Britain's first modern police force in London, nicknamed the 'Peelers'.

Nickname: *Orange Peel.*

Reason: Bob was against equality for Catholics, especially in Ireland. Anti-Catholics were called Orangemen – so Orange Peel – geddit?

Viscount Palmerston

Prime Minister: 1851–1865

Claim to fame: Saving Britain from disaster in the Crimean War.

Nickname: *Lord Cupid.*

Reason: He had an eye for the ladies and several love affairs.

The Victorian novel _Dracula_ was inspired by a real Romanian prince

Are you a bloodthirsty vampire fan? Do you devour the _Twilight_ movies or wish you could fight alongside Buffy the Vampire Slayer? Then you have Bram Stoker to thank.

Come here you lovely, tasty Victorians!

His gothic horror novel _Dracula_ was published in 1897 and started the STORM of stories about undead evil that surrounds us today.

But who was the inspiration behind Bram's Victorian monster?

⭐ And the truth is...

The Victorians loved gothic horror novels. *Varney the Vampire*; *Wagner the Wehr-wolf* and *Dr Jekyll and Mr Hyde* were all bestsellers during Victorian times. So Bram Stoker knew he was onto a winner when he based his monster on Vlad IV, the Prince of Wallachia (1431–1477).

Wallachia is part of modern-day Romania, but was a separate country in the 15th century. Vlad's unlucky subjects gave him two nicknames:

1. ***Dracula*** — 'the son of the Dragon or the Devil'

Actually the reason for this name wasn't too bad. Vlad's father was named 'the Dragon' because he had a fire-breathing beast painted on his shield. Not surprisingly, the average Wallachian peasant had never seen a picture of a dragon before BUT it looked very like an image they knew from church — the Devil.

2. ***Vlad the Impaler***

This second nickname was far more frightening! In a nutshell, anyone who opposed Prince Vlad's rule was stuck (or impaled) on a large wooden stake and left to die slowly as gravity pushed the point ever deeper into their body. Gruesome. And, you might say, a VERY sticky end! (Sorry...)

So to the Victorian novelist's mind, Vlad the Impaler was JUST the chap to bring back from the dead and terrorise Victorian England! By the way, you can sink your fangs into a tasty Dracula quiz on page 37.

Verdict:

VILE VICTORIANS!

Séance Crazy

The Victorian craze of spiritualism hit a peak in the 1870s. Spiritualists believed that it was possible to communicate with the spirits of the dead through séances (gatherings of people who are attempting to communicate with spirits of the dead)!

Thousands of Victorians paid to attend séances led by famous mediums – people who claimed to possess supernatural powers – like Florence Cook.

Séances were held in darkened rooms where mediums would summon beings from the afterlife. Florence Cook once called up a 'spirit child', Pocha, who famously stole money and trinkets from the audience!

A favourite trick of mediums was to exude ectoplasm from their mouths or noses. Ectoplasm was a white, eerie substance that allegedly made the shape of the being the medium was in touch with.

One word: Eeek!

The Victorians were obsessed with ghost hunting

The Victorians are remembered for their brilliant technology, but, boy, were they a superstitious lot! If a person died, the mirrors in their house were covered so the deceased's spirit wasn't trapped in the glass. And corpses were carried out of the house feet first, to stop them looking back and beckoning someone after them.

So is it true that the Victorians were obsessed with ghosts?

★ And the truth is...

Absolutely! If a place was rumoured to be haunted, out came the crowds to witness it. Bermondsey, then a ramshackle area of London, was a particular ghostly hot spot.

In 1868 a body was fished out of the River Thames and taken to the dead-house (where bodies were stored). Rumour spread that the corpse was seen walking by the river, and 2,000 people turned up to witness the spectre!

Séances, Ouija boards, mediums and apparitions were all the rage, too. In short, the Victorians loved anything spiritual!

Verdict:  ———————— TRUTH ————————

George Stephenson was
a reckless driver

Railway travel in Victorian days could be very risky. If you were hit by a train it would take more than a top hat to save you!

ACCIDENT LOG

Date: 15th September 1830.

Event: The opening of the first passenger railway line in the world, travelling from the city of Liverpool to Manchester, UK.

Victim: William Huskisson, MP for Liverpool.

Killer Blow: Delivered by the 4.5-ton locomotive, the **Rocket**.

Driver: George Stephenson, the most famous railway engineer of his day.

Well, this looks like an open and shut case — but was the famous engineer really a dodgy driver?

⭐ And the truth is...

The death of William Huskisson was the first railway fatality to be widely reported. When William's train stopped to take on water, he left the safety of his carriage to do some political schmoozing. He walked along outside the train to shake hands with the Duke of Wellington... and failed to spot the *Rocket* thundering towards him on the adjoining track.

William tried to scramble into the Duke's carriage, but the door of the carriage swung open — leaving him hanging directly in the path of the oncoming locomotive. He fell in front of the train and his leg was badly crushed. He died a few hours later.

Verdict: **BUSTED**

The Victorians led the internet revolution

The internet
is arguably the greatest modern
invention, but it was the Victorians who set up the first
electronic information highway — the telegraph system — over
150 years ago.

So did the Victorians start the internet revolution?

★ And the truth is...

The telegraph was a network of copper wires that ran alongside
railway lines. Messages were sent as electronic pulses, usually in
Morse Code — or dots and dashes — invented by the American,
Samuel Morse in 1840.

The first telegraph line opened in 1839 in London, undersea
telegraph cables reached Europe in 1850, and they went across
the Atlantic in 1858. The first telegraph line across the USA was
opened on 24th October 1861, putting the 'cowboy'-powered
Pony Express out of business just two days later.

Verdict:  TRUTH

FLABBERGASTATION!

I say!

IT'S CRIMINAL, I TELL YOU!

The Victorians had some downright creepy criminals.
Get a load of these dodgy types!

Cracksmen: Burglars who could get into any house
with their specialist tools — a jemmy (crowbar), betties
(lock picks) and a knife (for cutting glass).

Garrotters: Street robbers who worked in pairs.
One grabbed the victim round the throat while another rifled
through their pockets.

Pickpockets: The most skilled pickpockets were called
'mobsmen'. 'Buzzers' picked gentlemen's pockets while
'wires' specialised in stealing from ladies.

River Rats: Charming fellows who stripped the bodies
of those drowned in rivers! They took money, jewellery, shoes
and even gold teeth.

Sneaksmen: Chance thieves who stole goods on
display outside shops, or luggage from carts or coaches.

But, surprisingly, Victorian towns were relatively safe
compared to cities today. The murder rate was very low
— less than one or two murders per 100,000 people.

Greenwich Mean Time made people's lives shorter

How would you feel if your life was shortened by 10 minutes? Just like that — poof — gone! You'd be miffed. And so were many Victorians living outside London during Victorian times. They were stuck with Greenwich Mean Time. And it felt...well... pretty mean!

So what was going on?

⭐ And the truth is...

In the early 19th century every town had a local time, worked out with a sundial and the longitude of the location. Longitude is a geographical measurement, using imaginary lines running from the North to the South Poles.

The Royal Observatory in Greenwich set longitude for the world — the Prime Meridian, Longitude 0° 0' 0''. Every place on the Earth is measured in terms of its distance east or west from this line.

The Prime Meridian gave London accurate time and other towns adjusted their clocks according to the movement of the sun from Greenwich. So Bristol in the west of England was 10 minutes behind London, while Norwich in eastern England was several minutes ahead.

This was no problem when travel was slow, but the newly developing railway network needed a standard time. How could trains run to a timetable if every station had a different time? Think of the accident risk as the lines became busier!

In 1840 the Great Western Railway was the first to use London time for timetables, station clocks and train guards' watches. Other railway companies soon followed. By 1855 most British towns had given in and adopted GMT or Greenwich Mean Time.

GMT was essential for an age of fast change, but some people felt they had lost part of their local identity!

Verdict: **BUSTED** (but a teeny bit of TRUTH, too!)

only the rich could afford a 'penny farthing' bike

In Victorian times, the large penny (1d) and the small farthing (1/4d) were two of the lowest value coins. You could buy a loaf of bread for a penny, or a few sweets for a farthing.

But what's this got to do with bicycles, you may ask?

And the truth is...

The penny farthing was a popular bicycle from the 1870s to the 1890s. The front wheel was huge, anything up to 6 feet (2 metres) in diameter. The small back wheel added stability. The bikes were usually called 'high wheelers' and the nickname penny farthing (after the coins) didn't catch on until the 1890s.

Despite their weird looks, these bikes were expensive and were produced using cutting-edge technology. In the days before chains and gears the pedals were on the wheels, so the larger the wheel, the faster and more comfortable the bike. Even so they were hard to ride and if a cyclist 'took a header', (i.e. fell off!) they could be very seriously hurt.

A penny farthing bike cost between £30—£50 which was over six months' wages for an ordinary person! So to start with at least, cycling was a hobby mainly for wealthy gentlemen.

Verdict:

 ## BONUS FACT!

American Thomas Stevens cycled around the world on his penny farthing between 1884–1886. He started in San Francisco, made the first crossing of the USA on a bike to Boston – and just kept on going. In total Thomas travelled 13,500 miles (21,700 km). Most of the time he wore a military pith helmet (made of cork) in case he fell off. Sensible chap!

It sounds delicious, and full of soupy goodness
— but was a pea souper all it was cracked up to be?

★ And the truth is...

During the Victorian era, London became the largest city in the world, and the capital of the British Empire. The population rocketed from 1 million in 1800 to 6.7 million in 1900.

Millions of coal-fired chimneys from homes, workshops and factories belched thick smoke into the atmosphere. On windless days the smoke mixed with fog rolling off the River Thames to form poisonous smogs.

The air became thick with soot particles, tasted acrid and had a yellow or green tinge. In 1893, a smog lasted for three days and more than a thousand people died from bronchitis and other breathing problems.

Londoners called the smogs 'pea soupers' because they were often thick and green — just like, erm, pea soup!

Verdict: **BUSTED**

Victorian girls glowed in the dark

During Victorian times, matches had a phosphorus tip, so they lit easily — but at what cost to the people who worked in the match factories?

 ## And the truth is...

Phosphorus was a poisonous chemical. There was enough in a packet of matches to kill anyone who ate the heads. (And yes some people did eat them — either to commit suicide — or even sillier — because they liked the taste).

The Bryant and May match factory in London employed more than 1,500 women and girls in the 1880s. Girls as young as 13 worked 12-hour shifts for just four shillings (20p) a week.

But because of the chemicals used in the production of matches, many girls suffered from 'phossy jaw', caused by breathing in the vapour from the phosphorus. This awful disease started with toothache and swollen gums but soon became much worse. Infected jaws glowed an eerie green in the dark and eventually caused blood poisoning and death.

Verdict: _____ [a sad] TRUTH

> ## 'Made in Britain' was a proud Victorian boast

The age of amazing technology you now live in began around 300 years ago with the Industrial Revolution. Revolution means a huge change, and industrial means using machines. Put them together and... BOOM!

In 1700 most people lived and worked in the countryside, but over the next 150 years this traditional lifestyle was turned upside down by a wave of new ideas, inventions and technologies. Was this really the age of Made in Britain?

★ And the truth is...

As factories and workshops were built, people flocked to the booming towns to find work. The 1851 census showed that for the first time anywhere in the world, more people lived in towns and cities than in the countryside.

By 1850 Britain was called the 'workshop of the world'. British workers produced more than half the planet's coal, iron and steel and cotton. If foreign buyers wanted a ship, a railway engine or a machine tool they ordered it from a British business.

But Britain wasn't top dog for long. By the 1860s her industrial might was already challenged by the USA and Germany.

Verdict:  _____

Victorian housewives were regarded as 'angels'

The poet Coventry Patmore wrote in 1856 that the woman he loved was 'the angel in the house'. And this became a popular view of how women should behave in the 'ideal' Victorian family — be meek, charming, graceful, unselfish and obedient.

★ And the truth is...

In most Victorian families, the man of the house was in charge. He was expected to provide for his family and earn enough money to pay the bills. In middle-class families women rarely worked. The job of a wife was to keep her husband happy, manage the household and look after the children.

Women had very few rights in Victorian families. Until 1882, when a woman married her possessions became her husband's property — even if she had worked for them or inherited them from her own family!

Jobs for women

In many working-class families both the husband and wife had to work to make ends meet. The censuses — national surveys of the population taken every ten years — tell us a lot about Victorian workers.

The 1881 Census revealed that:

✳ 11 million people had jobs – and three million of those people were women.

✳ 1,300,000 women worked as domestic servants.

✳ 500,000 women worked in the textile industry, largely in cotton mills in Lancashire.

✳ 6,000 women worked as typists.

Trust me, Bertie, I know!

You are an angel, Flora.

Many women were treated like slaves not 'angels' — while others had no choice but to go out to work!

Verdict: ___ **BUSTED** ___

Having a baby was more dangerous than working in a coal mine

In the UK today, around 20 people die from falling out of bed every year — with children most at risk. So there's a one-in-two million chance of dying getting out of bed. Hmm, seems like a great excuse to lie in to us! But coal mining in Victorian times — now THAT sounds dangerous. And it was...

In 1875 around 500,000 men worked in coal mines. They faced dangers like being blown to bits by explosive gases or crushed by falling rocks. About 1,000 miners died in accidents each year — that's a one-in-500 chance of being killed in a colliery.

Compared to coal mining, how risky could childbirth be?

★ And the truth is...

In the 1870s almost 10% of mothers died either giving birth or from complications, such as infections, within a few weeks of labour. That's a one-in-10 risk.

So childbirth in Victorian times was far more dangerous than coal mining!

Verdict: ── TRUTH ──

FLABBERGASTATION!

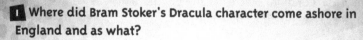

I say!

QUIZ!

Quench your bloodlust and discover what kind of vampire super-fan you are with this Dracula quiz!

1 Where did Bram Stoker's Dracula character come ashore in England and as what?

2 As well as Vlad the Impaler, which leading actor inspired the character of Dracula?

3 In 1897 what kind of 'modern technologies' did Bram Stoker's vampire hunters use?

Paupers were punished by having their heads shaved

Hundreds of huge workhouses were built in Britain from the 1830s onwards. If the poor (called paupers in Victorian times) wanted help, they had to give up their freedom and live in a workhouse. Conditions were harsh — but did they really punish people by shaving off all their hair?

★ And the truth is...

Often life in a workhouse depended on how strictly it was run by the Master and Matron — the people in charge. If they were cruel or lazy, conditions there could be appalling. Records show that at one UK workhouse in 1845, the paupers were so hungry that they gnawed the rotting meat from old bones brought in to be crushed for fertiliser.

However, most paupers were given enough to eat — although this often included a bowl of gruel — a sort of watery porridge with onions — a day. Even better, workhouse children were sent to school, and there was a doctor for the sick.

Paupers DID have their heads shaved, but not as a punishment for being poor. They were shaved because their hair was infested with lice!

Verdict: — a bit... BUSTED —

Punishments for the Poor

There were lots of rules in a workhouse. Paupers had to wear a uniform and were only allowed out with the Master's permission. Families were broken up, and slept in separate wards for men, women and children. If they disobeyed or broke the rules, the inmates could be punished. This is an extract from a real Pauper Offence book from Dorset:

Name	Offence	Date	Punishment
Elliott, Benjamin	Neglect of work	31 May 1842	Dinner withheld, and only bread for supper.
Rowe, Sarah	Noisy and swearing	19 June 1842	Locked up for 24 hours on bread and water.
Mintern, George	Fighting in school	26 July 1842	No cheese for one week.
Bartlett, Mary	Breaking window	21 Mar 1843	Sent to prison for 2 months.
Johnson, John	Refusing to work	19 Oct 1858	Cheese & tea stopped for supper. Breakfast stopped altogether.

> # Work done by the poor in the workhouse was worthless

The name says it all. The poor who went into a workhouse were often unemployed, but they certainly weren't allowed to sit around all day — the inmates were kept busy.

But did the work they did in the workhouse have a purpose?

★ And the truth is...

Victorian workhouses covered some of their running costs by making the poor do housekeeping and repairs. Women and girls scrubbed the floors and did the laundry while men did painting and decorating.

Other jobs brought in a small income to the workhouse, but were done mainly to keep the poor on the go. These included:

Oakham Picking: This riveting job involved slowly teasing apart old ropes. The fibres were mixed with tar and used for packing the timbers of wooden ships to make them watertight.

Stone Breaking: This back-breaking task involved breaking big stones into smaller stones used for surfacing roads.

Wood Chopping: Workhouse inmates were forced to chop wood to sell as sticks for lighting coal fires in Victorian houses.

Verdict: (Mainly) **BUSTED**

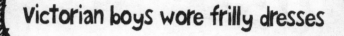

Victorian boys wore frilly dresses

Look at any Victorian family photo and you will see that girls and boys wore very similar clothes until roughly the age of five. Boys' outfits included pleated dresses and blouses, so it was very difficult to tell girls and boys apart.

Did Victorian parents have a penchant for dresses, or was there a simpler and more practical explanation?

★ And the truth is...

This type of unisex dressing didn't start with the Victorians. Young boys and girls had been dressed alike since at least the Middle Ages.

In the days before nappies it was easier to toilet train and clean children in dresses. Furthermore, parents weren't bothered about dressing their children according to gender. Boys and girls even wore the same coloured clothes. The 'blue for a boy, pink for a girl' idea only came along in the mid 20th century.

Boys were given their first pair of trousers at the age of five in a custom known as 'breeching'. But until that time, boys wore dresses, just like girls.

Verdict: ————

Crinoline Cages

Victorian ladies simply LOVED a wide skirt. In the 1840s skirts were pushed out by as many as six starched and stiffened petticoats. These became so heavy that walking was difficult, sweaty and uncomfortable. The heavy skirts often caused painful welts or grazes on the ladies' hips and waist.

In the 1850s the Americans invented the crinoline. This was a lightweight metal cage that hung from a band around the waist. Now skirts could be EVEN WIDER. Fashionable women became 'dome shaped' and it was impossible for two ladies to walk together though a door without crashing into each other.

In 1885 Sarah Ann Hedley jumped off the Clifton Suspension Bridge in Bristol after a lovers' tiff. It was reported that she survived because an updraft of air turned her crinoline skirt into a crude parachute, which meant that her fall was slower and she survived!

Blast this floating skirt!

The Victorian age was powered by electricity

Surely not, we hear you say! The Victorian era was the Age of Steam. Coal from the mines powered steam locomotives and ships, traction engines and factory machinery!

So what are we getting all steamed up about? Can we REALLY also credit the Victorians with pioneering electricity?

 And the truth is...

Yes, by Jove we can! By the 1870s the Victorians' inventive genius was bubbling over again. Take a look at this 'electric' list of Victorian achievements:

The first electric underground line opened in London in 1890.

Joseph Swan demonstrated the first electric light bulb in Newcastle, UK in 1879.

The modern turbine for generating electricity was invented by UK's Charles Parsons in 1884.

The first electric tram line opened in Brighton, UK in 1883.

In conclusion, the early Victorian era WAS steam powered but by 1900 electricity was widely used in homes, industry and transport!

Verdict: **TRUTH** and **BUSTED**

The poor washed their clothes in urine

Do you remember when your younger brother or sister was being toilet trained? If so, then you'll know all about pongs. But the Victorians lived constantly in a world of foul smells from drains, cesspits or polluted rivers — and among the pongiest was the smell of the poor.

The worst-paid families lived in grim, overcrowded slums. Often 30 or more people shared a toilet; water had to be carried from a tap in the street and people had to pay for water by the bucket, so many families could not afford it.

'Oh no! We're downwind of the washing!'

But is it true that the poor resorted to washing their clothes in such a drastic way?

And the truth is...

One way to save money on laundry was to make a simple cleaner from old wee. The family urine was stored in stone bottles until it was very strong. This was called 'wash' and used to clean clothes. Unfortunately it stank of ammonia, which is the sharp-smelling chemical in urine that acts as the 'cleaning agent'.

Wee has been used as a cleaner since at least Roman times. It does a good job, but the clothes need to be rinsed out thoroughly — with lots and lots of (expensive!) water.

The Victorian poor were known as 'the great unwashed', but this seems a bit unfair since it was their efforts to keep clean that created the nastiest smell.

Victorian doctors kept special hard, washable chairs in their surgeries for the poorest patients, and teachers needed strong stomachs for classes of Victorian slum children.

Verdict: _(a bit whiffy, but)_  TRUTH

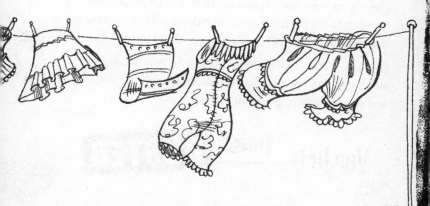

Queen Victoria lived in a beautiful palace made of crystal

The Crystal Palace was originally built in London's Hyde Park, and at the time was a staggering piece of building technology and design. Queen Victoria adored the Crystal Palace. She wrote in her diary in 1851:

'We remained two hours and a half and I came back with my head bewildered from the myriads of wonderful things.'

Victoria was a Queen. Queens live in palaces. This was a palace — but did Victoria live there, and was it really made of crystal?

★ And the truth is...

The Crystal Palace was a brilliant design by Joseph Paxton — a prefabricated building of iron and giant sheets of plate glass, definitely not crystal! It was built in 1851 to host the Great Exhibition, organised by Prince Albert to celebrate and showcase the different goods made by British industry.

There were more than 19,000 exhibits, from a huge steam hammer to the famous Koh-i-Noor diamond (once the largest diamond in the world).

So, sorry to bust the myth but the Crystal Palace was an exhibition hall not a palace, Queen Victoria didn't live in it and it was made of glass not crystal!

Verdict: _____ (Totally)  _____

FLABBERGASTATION!

THE GREAT CRYSTAL PALACE BIRD POO CRISIS!

I say!

Conservation Challenge 1

Building Site:	Hyde Park
Issue:	Giant elms on the building site need preserving.
Solution:	Build the Crystal Palace around them. The elms become a feature of the Great Exhibition.
Result:	Everyone is happy until...

Conservation Challenge 2

Issue:	Thousands of sparrows nest in the elms, pooping on the exhibits.
Solution 1:	Poison, but this has little effect.
Solution 2:	Queen Victoria consults the Duke of Wellington. His famous reply: 'Use Sparrowhawks, Ma'am.'
Result:	Sparrowhawks (a type of bird of prey) are flown in the Exhibition halls. The nesting sparrows flee!

Five-year-old boys made excellent chimney sweeps

It's been a long winter. The chimney of your Victorian house is clogged up with thick, black soot from burning coal fires to keep the parlour warm. You send for the chimney sweep and when he arrives he brings a little five-year-old boy with him. Then, to your horror, he pushes the lad up the chimney!

Surely, you gasp, this is a mistake?

★ And the truth is...

In Victorian times the sweep was the boss, but the hard, dirty work was done by young boys known as 'chummies'. The sweeps liked skinny boys because their thin bodies could easily shin up the narrow, twisting chimneys. These sweep masters weren't kind. They rubbed salt in the boys' cuts to toughen up the skin, and beat them if they made a mess. If the boys got stuck, the sweeps stuck pins in their feet to get them moving.

To make matters worse, thick soot fell into their eyes and noses, leaving them blind, choking and unable to breathe. Some chummy boys suffered lung diseases or suffocated to death. Others suffered terrible burns when the chimney was still hot, or fell to their deaths when they lost their footing.

If a boy worked for years he risked 'the black spit' or 'soot wart' cancers, caused by exposure to soot.

Verdict: _____

The Victorians turned dog poo into pure gold

Nowadays we know that well-trained dog owners scoop their dogs' poop. It's hygienic; it's socially responsible, and it's better for people and the environment. But in Victorian times, people picked up dog poo for a totally different reason. But could dog poo really be turned into 'pure' gold?

⭐ And the truth is...

In Victorian times, 'pure' was the slang name for dog poo that was used in the leather or tanning industry to treat and condition animal hides. Even the delicate leather that was used to bind books had been treated with dog faeces. Poo-eee!

In 1850s London, 'pure finders' were people who made a living by walking the streets and collecting buckets full of fresh dog poop. Some scooped the poop with a glove, but others used their hands, since it was easier to wash their hands than a glove.

The pure finders earned a tiny amount of money from the tanneries for each bucket of poo they collected. The tanners preferred dry-ish poo because it was more alkaline, and therefore made the leather more supple!

Verdict: _____ (a very stinky) **TRUTH**

The Royal Navy Stamped on Slavery

In the 18th century Britain was the top slave-trading country, until a slow change of heart led to the abolition of slavery in 1807.

During the Victorian years the Royal Navy fought the battle to end slavery. In the 1840s the West African Squadron – around 25 ships and 2,000 men – chased and captured slave ships from the USA, Spain, Brazil and Portugal.

In 1841, for example, HMS Acorn seized the Spanish slaving and pirate ship Gabriel. Freed slaves were usually released in Sierra Leone, Africa.

These anti-slavery patrols were one of the Royal Navy's greatest achievements.

Victorian photographers were the first to say 'cheese'

The first photograph was taken in Britain in about 1835 by Henry Fox Talbot. Early Victorian cameras were large, complicated and expensive, so most photographs were taken in a studio.

Going to the photographer was a special occasion — perhaps a once-in-a-lifetime visit! Everyone dressed in their best clothes and had to keep very still — sometimes for minutes at a time — or the photograph would risk being blurred.

So what did Victorian photographers get their clients to say while posing in their studios, to ensure a good picture?

⭐ And the truth is...

OK, for a start let's get the untruth out of the way. Apparently, they DIDN'T say:

Cheese

Go on, say it... CHEEEESE. Saying 'cheese' stretches your mouth into the shape of a smile. But smiling in photos wasn't the fashion until the 20th century.

What they DID get their clients to say was:

Prunes

Your turn again... say PROOONES. In Victorian times, a small, pursed mouth was considered beautiful... and so the word 'prunes' did the trick.

An alternative to this was:

Watch the Birdie

Most Victorian photographers had something to keep children amused and help them sit still. Watching a toy bird kept the little shufflers from wriggling about too much!

Verdict:  BUSTED

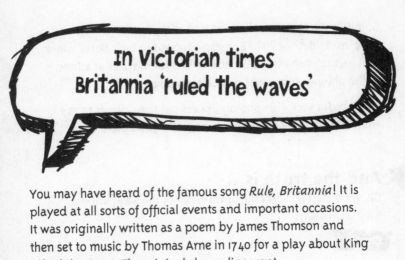

In Victorian times
Britannia 'ruled the waves'

You may have heard of the famous song *Rule, Britannia!* It is played at all sorts of official events and important occasions. It was originally written as a poem by James Thomson and then set to music by Thomas Arne in 1740 for a play about King Alfred the Great. The original chorus line went:

Rule, Britannia! Britannia, rule the waves!

However, by Victorian times the song lyrics had changed to:

Rule, Britannia! Britannia, rules the waves!

Why was that extra 's' important?

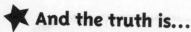

★ And the truth is...

After the Battle of Trafalgar in 1805, Britain had the most powerful navy in the world. The century following this, until the First World War, is sometimes called Pax Britannica, or the British peace. This was enforced by the Royal Navy all over the world.

Navies don't come cheap. The first iron battleship, HMS *Warrior*, joined the fleet in 1861 and cost £377,000, but Britain could afford to pay for such expensive ships.

At the time Britain was known as the 'workshop of the world'. The nation's import and export trade jumped from £80 million in 1801 to nearly £1.5 billion in 1901. Meanwhile the British Empire grew to span the globe — covering 11 million square miles (17.7 million square km), with a population of more than 390 million people!

By 1893 the Royal Navy had 76,000 men, 35 battleships and 158 smaller warships. Their job was to protect British trade routes, like the Suez Canal, and safeguard the Empire.

But what about that sneaky little 's' on the end of 'rules'?

It changed the meaning of the song from 'It's our job to grow strong enough to rule the waves'... to... 'We know we rule the waves.' Wow.

Verdict: —————— TRUTH ——————

Victorian soldiers wore red uniforms to hide the blood

British soldiers wore red uniforms in battle from the 1640s to the 1880s, and were known across the world as Redcoats. Was this a cunning plan to hide the blood of wounded soldiers and make them seem tougher? And if so, why did the Victorian army finally give up red uniforms?

★ And the truth is...

Red uniforms don't hide blood, that's one of history's myths. Blood shows up as a black stain on most fabrics, including red ones. The Victorian army wore red because that was the colour of British uniforms during the Battle of Waterloo in 1815.

Victorian generals were proud of their past, so they felt that a red uniform for their soldiers should stay. A quarter of a million British troops fought in the Crimean War from 1853—1856; most in red battledress.

The thing that finally forced a change in uniform colour was new weaponry. Modern armies replaced their short-range muskets with long-range rifles — making a soldier in a red coat an easy target. By the 1880s most troops wore khaki uniforms to blend in with mud and dust and generally act as camouflage.

Verdict: — BUSTED —

Bloodybacks

As well as Redcoats, the British army had other, less pleasant, nicknames. Some regiments were known as 'bloodybacks' because their officers flogged (or beat) their soldiers so often.

Army discipline was very strict:

✳ Victorian soldiers were flogged after a court-martial (an army trial led by a senior officer). Court-martial offences included disobeying an order, drunkenness, sleeping on duty or going AWOL (absent without leave).

✳ The whip used to flog the soldiers was a 'cat o' nine tails' – a rope with up to nine loose strands, each dense enough to cut through skin.

✳ In 1829, army law was changed to allow no more than 300 strokes, but this was still enough to kill a soldier if the flogging wasn't properly supervised by an army doctor.

✳ The number of strokes was reduced to 50 in 1847, but flogging wasn't abolished until 1881.

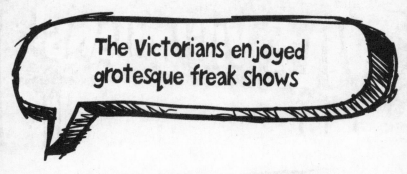

The Victorians loved travelling fairgrounds and circuses. People flocked to ride the roundabouts, visit fortune tellers, gasp at performing animals and gawp at the freak shows. Pardon? 'Gawp at the freak shows'? What exactly was going on?

★ And the truth is...

It seems cruel today but the 19th century was the heyday of freak shows. Victorians queued to see deformities of all kinds. These included so-called giants, dwarves, obese people, extremely thin people, those with malformed limbs or excessive hair, and conjoined twins.

Some acts became famous such as Chang and Eng, who were conjoined twins joined at the chest, or General Tom Thumb, who was only 64cm tall. When Tom Thumb married Lavinia Warren, who was 81cm high, their wedding was front-page news across Europe and the USA.

This all seems very cruel now, but many freak show acts apparently enjoyed stage life. They had the support of other performers and often earned good wages — as much as £20 a week in the 1890s (equivalent to around £1,250 now). The money gave them the kind of freedom and independence they could never have had in ordinary life.

Life in a freak show was considered so attractive that some ordinary people wanted to join in. Set on fame, they made themselves look different enough to be hired as an act — perhaps by tattooing the majority of their skin, growing their hair down to their knees or learning how to be super-bendy contortionists!

Verdict:

The Empire provided the English language with some great words

Having a *curry* for supper, before *shampooing* your hair and putting on your *pukka pyjamas*? Or leaving the comfort of your *bungalow* to don some *khaki dungarees* and sail a *dinghy* down a *jungle* river?

Congratulations! Using such vocabulary makes you a true child of the Empire!

★ And the truth is...

The Victorians picked up thousands of words from the peoples they conquered and added them to the English language, making it more diverse, varied and colourful.

These words came from the Indian Empire — modern India, Pakistan and Bangladesh:

chintz chutney curry dinghy
dungarees gymkhana juggernaut
jungle khaki loot pukka pyjamas
shampoo teak thug veranda yoga

Verdict: ——————— TRUTH ———————

In Scotland sheep were more important than people

Have you ever had a holiday in the Scottish Highlands and Islands and wondered why this beautiful, vast area is so... empty. Why do so few people live there?

Before 1755 over half the people of Scotland lived in the Highlands. Most Highlanders spoke Gaelic, a language similar to Irish, and made a living through farming.

The Duke of Sutherland, a powerful landowner, owned vast areas of the Highlands. To 'improve' his lands, he began to replace farmers with sheep. By 1820 he had nearly 120,000 sheep!

★ And the truth is ....

150,000 people were driven from the Sutherland estates. Often their homes were burned and their cattle driven away. Children and old people starved or froze to death in the ruins.

Tens of thousands of Highlanders were persuaded — or forced — to emigrate to Canada or Australia. By 1850 around 50,000 had emigrated to Cape Breton Island in Nova Scotia alone.

The Highland Clearances were one of the most shameful events of early Victorian times.

Verdict: A damning TRUTH

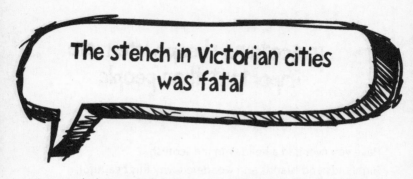

The stench in Victorian cities was fatal

Victorian ladies rarely left the house without small bags of dried flowers clutched to their nose. They carried them to hide the nasty whiffs that lurked outside — niffs so strong that many doctors feared they were poisonous enough to kill. What was causing these sensational stinks, and were they really deadly?

★ And the truth is...

☆ *Stinks kill*

It was not until the 1880s that most doctors believed microorganisms caused disease. Before that, the answer seemed obvious — bad smells. According to the miasma theory, dangerous gases from rotting matter caused infections.

And Victorian cities were festering nests of putrefaction. Broken sewers, dung heaps, horse droppings, pigsties, cowsheds, butchers' waste and black, polluted rivers all combined to create an 'infernal stench'.

☆ *Wrong but right*

The miasma theory was wrong, but even so it inspired health reformers like Edwin Chadwick and William Farr to campaign for a clean up. To them a bad smell was a murderer at large — a very successful murderer. One child in every five died before their fifth birthday, many from drinking polluted water.

Most towns looked to London and the projects of engineer Joseph Bazalgette to show the way. In the 1840s, raw sewage flowed freely through the streets of the capital and ended up in the River Thames — an estimated 250 tons of poo a day.

Between 1858 and 1865 Bazalgette organised a workforce of 6,000 to rebuild the capital's sewers. More than 82 miles (132 km) of brick main sewers were built to take the outflows from 1,100 miles (1,800 km) of new street sewers.

Verdict: — **BUSTED** —

(but cleaning up the causes of the stinks saved lives!)

Many Victorian children died before their fifth birthday

Victorian children lived close to death — with a one-in-five chance of not making it past their fifth birthday. Most had lost brothers or sisters to diseases like diarrhoea, whooping cough or diphtheria. Child death affected both rich and poor families, but did they cry about it? No, not at all.

★ And the truth is...

Death was a fact of life for the Victorians. Families often had lots of children, so they mourned their dead and moved on. Children knew that life might be short and this showed in their play. Here is a popular Victorian rhyme for a skipping game:

> Grandmother, Grandmother
> Tell me the truth
> How many years am I
> Going to live?
> One, Two, Three, Four...

Verdict: TRUTH

Victorian towns had more pigs than people

Population growth in many UK Victorian towns and cities was phenomenal. Just gasp at this table:

Town	1801	1851
Birmingham	71,000	233,000
Bradford	13,000	104,000
Manchester	75,000	303,000

Most people living in these 'boom towns' moved in from the countryside and brought country ways of life with them. So early Victorian cities were crammed full of animals such as chickens, cows, geese and pigs. Especially pigs.

Victorian slums were packed with pig pens but if there was no space, families simply brought the pigs home. In Notting Hill, in west London, pigs outnumbered people by three to one in 1850!

During the day the pigs were turned out to feed and, bizarrely, acted as street cleaners. They ate anything they could find including horse poo, human poo and, of course, their own poo!

Verdict:  TRUTH (depending on the area!)

VILE VICTORIANS!

Crossing Sweepers

Victorian streets had a problem – the great horse poo scandal. Every horse dropped around 7 kg of poo a day – and there were millions of horses in use, pulling wagons, taxis and trams. Result: piles of poo choking every road.

But here at Truth or Busted HQ, we say 'where there is poo there is work', and so did the Victorians! For the price of a simple broom, a poor Victorian could set themselves up with a job as a crossing sweeper.

The trick to being a successful crossing sweeper was to spot a well-dressed gentleman or lady looking to cross the road and clear a path through the mounds of horse poo for them. This was called a broom walk.

Most British crossing sweepers were young boys, but others were elderly or disabled.

Sweepers only earned about a shilling a day, but some city residents thought they were little better than beggars, referring to them as 'highway men with brooms in their hands'.

A hot bath was harmful to one's health

By the 1870s bathrooms with hot and cold running water began to appear in Victorian houses. But hot baths were considered bad for the health so they were rarely taken! Can this really be true?

★ And the truth is...

When Queen Victoria moved into Buckingham Palace in 1837 there wasn't a bathroom anywhere. The rich could easily afford to have bathrooms installed, but they didn't want to knock holes in their grand houses when servants could carry water for washing to any room they wanted.

Early Victorians believed that bathing stripped a protective layer from the skin, and it was decades before the idea was accepted that clean skin was healthy.

Hot baths in particular were treated with suspicion. *A Handbook for Ladies and Gentlemen*, published in 1860, warned that hot baths left the bather *'powerless and prostrate'* while a cold bath *'cleanses less but invigorates'*.

A cold bath it was then. Brrrrr!

Verdict: ————— TRUTH —————

'Spending a penny' was a luxury

We all know that spending a penny means going for... well, you know... a wee, a tinkle, a number 1, right?

But where did this strange phrase come from? Well, it's all the fault of George Jennings, a Brighton plumber. During the Great Exhibition in 1851 he was monkeying around with flush toilets but what exactly was he doing — and why was it such a luxury?

★ And the truth is....

George installed the first public flush toilets in the Retiring Rooms of the Crystal Palace.

He called them Monkey Closets. Visitors paid one penny to use them and get a touch of luxury. For 'spending a penny' they got a clean seat, a towel, a comb and a shoe shine.

During the exhibition 827,280 people used the toilets, which constituted 14% of all visitors. The busiest day was 8th October, with 11,171 paying customers!

Verdict: **TRUTH**

A Victorian innovation saved people from drowning in horse poo

In 1894 *The Times* newspaper predicted that by 1950 London would be 'nine feet (three metres) deep in horse muck'. Wowzer. Considering the height of the average person is nowhere near nine feet, this would indeed have resulted in 1950s' Londoners swimming in poo! Similarly, a New York commentator of the 1890s concluded that by 1930 the horse droppings on New York's streets would rise to Manhattan's third-story windows. Eeeww!

In the 1830s, 3,000,000 tons of horse poo were dropped on the streets of Victorian towns. By 1900 this had risen to 10,000,000 tons. By 1880, 50,000 horses were needed to pull London buses and trams alone. Every horse pooped between 7–15 kg a day.

Rainy weather turned city streets into poo swamps and rivers of muck. Dry weather was no better, as the horse manure turned to dust and was blown about by the wind, coating buildings in filth and choking poor pedestrians.

But did people ever come close to drowning in poo? Or did some amazing technical innovation come along during the Victorian era to prevent this from happening?

And the truth is...

Future generations of Londoners were saved by German Victorian Karl Benz, who built the world's first three-wheeled 'horseless carriage' or automobile in 1886. Cars soon became popular as hi-tech transport for the rich in Europe, and horses were gradually phased out as a mode of transport. The streets became cleaner and Londoners probably breathed a sign of relief! But British manufacturers had a big problem.

Old-fashioned 'Red Flag' laws meant that cars couldn't go faster than 3-4 miles (4.5-6.5 km) per hour, and weren't allowed out on the highways without a man walking in front and waving a red flag to warn oncoming horses. These laws were abolished in 1896 but it took years for British car makers to catch up with their foreign rivals.

Verdict: _____ TRUTH _____

If you have an infected cut today, you can pop along to the doctor for antibiotics to clear it up. No problem. But in Victorian times germs ran wild. Infection often led to gangrene, and perhaps a nasty amputation to stop blood poisoning spreading through the whole body.

The trouble was Victorian surgeons had no idea that bacteria were being passed to their patients by dirty instruments and unwashed hands. But did they really think it was fine to operate in blood-splattered old coats?

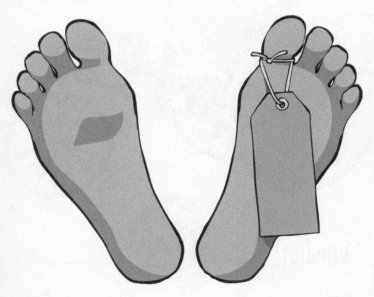

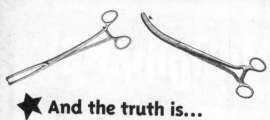

⭐ And the truth is…

At the start of Queen Victoria's reign (1837–1901) the only cure for a badly infected wound was a terrifying trip to the surgeon. Never mind no antibiotics — there were no anaesthetics to kill pain or antiseptics to prevent infections, either!

Surgeons worked with their patients awake and strapped to a wooden bench to stop them running away. They used scalpels or shears to cut through skin and flesh, and saws to get through bone. Working fast to limit blood loss, a good surgeon could amputate a leg in 90 seconds. But many unlucky patients died from shock in the meantime.

In a world far from today's ultra-clean operating theatres, Victorian surgeons wore their dirtiest coats — often soaked in blood from the last amputation. Come on — it makes perfect sense, doesn't it? Who in their right mind would want to spoil a nice, clean jacket?

⭐ BONUS FACT!

Top surgeon Joseph Lister was famous for the speed of his work. He could amputate a leg in 30 seconds!

Verdict: _____ (An infection-laden)  **TRUTH**

Milestones in Medicine

1844 American dentist **Horace Wells** used the gas nitrous oxide to anaesthetise his patients.

1846 The first British operation was carried out using ether (alcohol) as an anaesthetic. A newspaper headline at the time declared: *We Have Conquered Pain.*

1847 British doctor **James Simpson Young** used ether to help a woman through the pain of a difficult childbirth.

1854 John Snow proved that the disease cholera is spread by polluted water.

1860 Florence Nightingale set up the first British nursing school at St Thomas's Hospital, London.

1865 Joseph Lister used carbolic acid as an antiseptic during operations. His patient death rate fell from 46% to 15%.

The Victorians unleashed an army of teachers on innocent children

Until the Victorian era, it was only the wealthy who educated their children. Poorer families sent their children out to work in mills, factories, mines or domestic houses as soon as they could. In 1880 thousands of Victorian children were rounded up and forced to attend school. 'It's an outrage,' I hear you cry... Or was it?

 ## And the truth is...

The 1870 Education Act promised school places for every child between five and 10 years old, and in 1880 going to school was made compulsory.

After 1880 school attendance officers began to track down truants. This was called 'the great round up'. Between 1870 and 1888 the number of kids recorded on school registers shot up from 1,152,000 to 4,688,000.

To cope with all the children, the nation trained an army of teachers. In 1870 there were 37,714 teachers but by 1888 the number had soared to 100,914.

Verdict:

TRUTH

75

Victorian children started school with a clean slate

Blotted your copy book* at school? Never mind, teacher will let you start again with *a clean slate***. But where do these phrases come from?

⭐ And the truth is...

Younger children wrote with chalk on small slates, about the size of a tablet computer. Mistakes were rubbed out with a damp cloth or a wet finger. At the end of the day the pupils wiped off their work, so they could start the next day with...
ta-raaa!... **A CLEAN SLATE!**

Older pupils were allowed to use pens with nibs and ink. They practised handwriting in copy books every day. Each page had to be perfect, so woe betide any pupil who loaded too much ink on their nib and dropped a blob because...

...yep...you're right... they had **blotted their copy book.**

* *to do something that spoils other people's opinion of you.*
** *a chance to start over or start afresh.*

Verdict:  TRUTH

76

Victorian children were seen but not heard

In 2013 historians researched children's behaviour in public parks during the Victorian era and got quite a surprise.

In Victorian times, parks were built in the growing cities of Britain to give children somewhere green and healthy to play. Instead of grimy cobbled streets there were trees, grass and animals. Surely this would turn Victorian kids into little angels?

And the truth is...

Well, put it this way, Victorian park keepers in the new public parks didn't have time to sleep on the job! Children were reported for:

- ⭐ Chasing sheep and deer round the parks.
- ⭐ Sitting on park benches and shouting abuse at passers by.
- ⭐ Jumping over fences to paddle in the lakes.
- ⭐ Making rods to catch the ornamental fish.
- ⭐ Stealing fruit from the trees.

Verdict: ── **BUSTED** ──

Victorian children had a terrible time at school

The Victorian era could be harsh for schoolchildren. Corporal punishment (smacking, beating or flogging) was commonplace both at school and at home. Implements included the cane, the 'tawse' (a fringed leather strap) or the birch (made from twigs).

And the truth is...

On the one hand

Most Victorians believed that children needed discipline if they were to grow up to be responsible adults. Parents usually smacked their children if they misbehaved at home and expected teachers to do the same.

Teachers struggled to manage large classes, often with 40 or more children. To keep order, pupils were punished for breaking school rules like talking in class or arriving late, or, horror of horrors, disobeying an instruction.

Boys were caned on their bottoms and girls on their hands or the backs of their legs. Other punishments included a good telling off, kneeling on the hard floor with your hands behind your head, writing lines (copying the same sentence 50 or 100 times) or being made to wear the Dunce's Cap — a big hat with a D on it which signalled you as 'stupid'.

And on the other hand

Most children enjoyed long playtimes. Sorry girls, but boys' yards were often bigger because they were expected to play team games like cricket and football. Footballs didn't last long — they were often just an inflated pig's bladder begged from a butcher's shop.

Schools gave rewards including prizes for full attendance and good work. Classes were often taken out on trips, perhaps to the beach or a local park. On special occasions pupils were given treats such as bags of sweets, concerts or magic lantern shows.

Verdict: (A lot of) TRUTH (and a bit) BUSTED

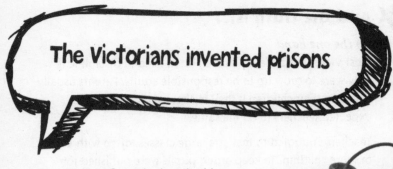

The Victorians invented prisons

Invented prisons? Surely there had been prisons around since ancient times...

Was there something different about the new prisons built by the Victorians?

 And the truth is...

Pre-Victorian prisons were overcrowded with men, women and children all locked up together. There was very little hope of criminals reforming, or sometimes even making it out alive.

The Victorians invented a new type of prison, designed to stop inmates mixing together. Prisoners were kept away from one another in small, separate cells. The idea was if criminals couldn't mix, they couldn't be a bad influence on one another.

Prisoners spent most of their time alone in their cells, and when they went into the exercise yards they wore masks to stop them recognising one another.

Inmates who were caught talking to each other were punished by spending hours walking the treadmill — a giant wooden wheel, just like an exercise wheel in a hamster cage.

Verdict: **BUSTED** (But they did improve prisons)

Jack the Ripper was the worst Victorian murderer

Between August and November 1888, five women were brutally murdered in Whitechapel, east London. The killer was never caught, but became known around the world as Jack the Ripper.

There have been films, books and TV series produced about this character, but was Jack the Ripper the worst murderer of the Victorian era?

⭐ And the truth is...

It's true that Jack was notorious. However, he wasn't exactly the worst Victorian murderer... Read on!

Amelia Dyer was a midwife with sinister motives. It was shameful to be an unmarried mother in Victorian times, so unmarried women paid Dyer to find foster parents for their babies. However, the unscrupulous woman took their money and killed the poor infants instead!

Dyer was hung at Newgate Prison in 1896 for the murder of a single baby by the name of Doris Marmon, but ongoing investigations led police to believe that she had murdered at least 200 and perhaps as many as 400 other babies over 20 years. So although you have probably never heard of her, Amelia Dyer was a far more prolific killer than Jack the Ripper!

Verdict: **BUSTED**

Some Victorian women ran 'baby farms'

Growing babies on farms — amazing but surely untrue! In fact, the reality was far sadder.

⭐ And the truth is...

Because unmarried Victorian mothers faced great shame, many women wanted to hide their babies away, as if they had never existed. To do this they turned to 'baby farms' — the nickname given to homes that took in unwanted children.

Some baby farmers promised to have the babies adopted by good families, while others agreed to care for them as long as the mother needed, all for a fee. Sometimes honest people made a living by looking after these poor children, but often the children in baby farms were neglected and died.

The famous Victorian writer Charles Dickens attacked the conditions in baby farms in his novel *Oliver Twist* (1838):

In eight and a half cases out of ten, either the child sickened from want and cold, or fell into the fire from neglect, or got half-smothered by accident; in any one of which cases, the miserable little being was usually summoned into another world.

Verdict: [a very sad] **TRUTH**

82

Victorian doctors used leeches to cure illnesses

Leeches are a type of thickish worm with two suckers at either end of their body. They live mainly in freshwater and feed on the blood of other creatures to survive. We all know the stories of leeches attaching themselves to the leg or arm of a poor soul who has decided to have a paddle in a river, but using them to purposely SUCK BLOOD from an ill person?

★ And the truth is...

During Victorian times, blood-letting was a common remedy for many illnesses. This involved a doctor bleeding a patient, because it was thought that 'bad blood' in the body was causing the disease.

First the doctor cut the patient's skin to make them bleed and applied a warm cup to draw out some of the blood. Live leeches were then used to suck the blood out of the patient's veins!

Verdict: _____ **TRUTH**

Dodgy Dictionary

The way people speak changes all the time and new words come in and out of fashion. But Victorian criminals, in particular, had some great expressions for describing their dodgy dealings:

barker – a gun

buster – a burglar

dipper – a pickpocket

going snowing – stealing washing from gardens

lagged – sent to jail

little snakesman – a small boy used to break in to houses

nark – an informer

niner – a prisoner serving a nine-year sentence

to put someone's light out – to kill someone

rattled – very drunk

salt box – the condemned cell

swag – stolen property

Victorian parents treated public hangings as a family day out

Punishments were strict in Victorian times and included public hangings, which went on until 1868. Hangings were gruesome events, and crowds gathered to picnic and watch the criminal meet their miserable end. But is it true that families treated it as a day out — and took their children along?

★ And the truth is...

In September 1853, *The Times* newspaper reported on a multiple hanging at Kirkland Jail in Liverpool. This event attracted around 100,000 spectators. A special train, 30 carriages long, took sightseers from Bradford in Yorkshire. The reporter noted:

The majority were respectably dressed – decent-looking mechanics, women in silk dresses and youths from the age of 12 to 20 years of age.

Public hangings always attracted huge crowds. Parents pushed their children to the front or sat them on their shoulders to get a good view. If they were bored, the younger children played games at the foot of the gallows!

Verdict:  TRUTH

VILE VICTORIANS!

Top Hangman

William Calcraft's CV

Occupation: Executioner to the City of London.

Pay: One guinea for each hanging.

First executions: 27th March 1829 he hanged Thomas Lister for burglary and George Wingfield for highway robbery.

Popularity: In great demand across the country.

Total deaths: 450 hangings.

Perks: Every hanging used a new rope. Gory souvenir hunters queued to buy pieces of rope from him by the inch!

Technique: The 'short-drop method'. Victims fell only three feet (90cm) and often died from strangulation rather than a broken neck.

Crowd pleaser: Climbing on the shoulders of prisoners to hasten death. (This always got boos or cheers)

Last execution: The hanging of James Godwin in 1874.

Victorians went to church religiously every Sunday

We've all been taught that Victorians thought of themselves as Christian people, and the vast majority of families (rich and poor) attended church devotedly every Sunday morning in their 'Sunday best' clothes and shiny, polished shoes. But was this really the case?

★ And the truth is...

Queen Victoria was an Anglican. She worshipped in churches belonging to the Church of England — and so did most rich and middle-class people. Other Christians, such as Methodists or Baptists, held simpler services in chapels.

But in 1851 the nation learned a shocking secret...

A census was taken of all the people who went to church on Sundays in England. And it showed that less than half the population of 18 million attended a service. Most ordinary working people were too busy earning a living.

Verdict: (Very) **BUSTED**

Football was a game for gentlemen players

Most people think that Victorian football was a working-class game. Is this 'back of the net' or an own goal?

★ And the truth is...

In the early 19th century, football was played by elite public schools like Eton, and universities like Cambridge. So when did posh football become people's football?

The Football Association was set up in 1863 to agree a common set of rules for the game. The first FA cup final was played in March 1872 between Wanderers and Royal Engineers.

Many of the early clubs were formed by old boys from public schools and for the first 11 years the FA cup was won by gentleman's clubs like Oxford University or Old Etonians.

But in 1883 there was a football earthquake. The cup was won by Blackburn Olympics, a team of iron foundry and cotton mill workers. Their supporters were described as *a northern hoard*.

Many of the great working-class clubs were founded in the 1870s, including Glasgow Rangers (1872), Birmingham City (1875) and Everton (1878), and soon started to make an impact on the game.

Verdict:  **TRUTH** (until the 1870s)

The Victorians were far too prim and proper to enjoy themselves

We've all seen films or TV shows set during the Victorian era. Tea with the vicar, an exciting game of cards or perhaps an evening of needlework was what passed for fun and entertainment in those days. Or was it?

★ And the truth is...

In the early years of Victoria's reign, the working classes had a wild old time.

Blood Sports

Cruel blood sports such as bull baiting, dog and cockerel fights pulled in huge, bloodthirsty crowds. The Cruelty to Animals Act was passed in 1835 so animal fights were held in secrets pits — far away from the patrols of the new police forces. Gambling on fights was heavy, and champion fighting dogs sold for hundreds of pounds.

Beer Houses

The Beer Act of 1830 allowed anyone to brew their own beer and sell it from their home — known as a 'beer house'. This was intended to stop people drinking strong gin in places called 'gin palaces'. Unfortunately, people were not aware of how bad alcohol is for the health or manners, and petty crimes like assaults, thefts and vandalism shot up.

Music Halls

Beer houses threatened the trade of pubs, so landlords hit back with music halls. The first music halls were set up in the 1830s as concert rooms in pubs. Audiences were charged a few pennies and could eat and drink while they watched all kinds of acts: singers, comedians, or even circus performers. Music hall audiences were notoriously wild — and many entertainers were booed off stage.

Verdict:  **BUSTED**

Victorian music halls were a disaster waiting to happen

From the 1850s music halls sprang up across the country offering a mixture of songs, comedy and speciality acts. Top stars included Marie Lloyd (a comedienne and singer) and Little Titch, a comedian who danced in 28-inch (90-cm) boots!

So was it the performers or the music halls themselves that were a disaster?

★ And the truth is...

The music hall stars were brilliant and highly popular, but the buildings themselves were accidents waiting to happen. Safety inspections were unheard of, emergency exits didn't exist and false fire alarms led to deadly mass panics!

Here are some examples:

- ✈ *1868 A faulty gas chandelier sparked a panic at a music hall in Manchester: 23 people were killed.*

- ✈ *1878 The ceiling at a Liverpool music hall fell down: 37 people were killed.*

- ✈ *1884 A fire alarm at a music hall in Glasgow caused a rush for the door: 14 people were killed.*

Verdict:  TRUTH

VILE VICTORIANS!

The Victoria Hall Disaster

Sunderland, northeast England, was the scene of the worst music hall disaster in memory. On 16th June 1883, **2,000 children crowded into the huge Victoria Hall** to watch a conjurer, Alexander Fay, and his 'enchantress' sister Annie.

The tickets came with the promise of prizes to be handed out as the audience left – toys or books for those with the right numbers. When the show was over, the prizes were handed out in the main auditorium – in full view of over **1,100 excited children** in the upstairs gallery. **Hundreds bolted for the stairs – and tragedy.**

The main exit door had been opened inwards with a gap of about 50cm to allow one person to leave at a time. Only one – so the tickets could be checked. As more and more children surged down the stairs, those at the bottom were **crushed by the sheer weight of the crowd.** Before the door could be smashed open, **183 had died.**

The survivors' tales were harrowing. Little William Codling remembered: **Soon we were most uncomfortably packed but still going down. Suddenly I felt that I was treading upon someone lying on the stairs and I cried in horror to those behind 'Keep back, keep back! There's someone down.'**

Where can I find myths about...